Faithfully Stepping Journal

Copyright © 2022 Amanda Manney

All rights reserved. No part of this book may be reproduced, stored in a retrieval system, or transmitted in any form or by any means—electronic, mechanical, photocopy, recording, or otherwise—without written permission from the publisher except for brief quotations in printed reviews.

Getting Started

The Faithfully Stepping Journal is the culmination of twenty years of Bible reading and study. I have used various journals, Bible study guides, and other types of notebooks over the years. Journaling is the key that has helped me grow the most in my walk with the Lord. A journal provides a place to record my prayers and devotional thoughts from what I read each day and becomes a great encouragement in discouraging times. Journaling daily will help to develop a consistency in your prayer life and Bible reading that will propel your spiritual growth to new levels.

Each day, you will have the opportunity to write down your thoughts and prayers. This journal uses an easy format to help you track your progress in your walk with God and will encourage you throughout the day. If you are like me, you will find your attitude will be dramatically different on the days you journal and the days you do not.

I like to journal in the morning, so I can take what I've read with me throughout the day. If you are a night person and like to spend time reading and praying before going to bed, I would journal at night and then read through your thoughts the next morning as a refresher.

By beginning a habit of daily journaling, you will find that the person you were a month ago is very different than the one you are today. The encouragement and guidance you will receive from spending time in God's Word will become like a fresh well of water that you will want to come back to every day. The renewal you will experience is exactly what Paul wrote about in Romans 12:2, *"And be not conformed to this world: but be ye transformed by the renewing of your mind, that ye may prove what is that good, and acceptable, and perfect, will of God."*

The nuts and bolts of the process are simple. There are many formats to organize your prayer and Bible reading. The Faithfully Stepping Journal is a simple guide to get you started.

Each day you will begin by recording the day and date. This will help you to track your progress and see which days you miss, so you can make adjustments to your schedule and ultimately become more consistent with journaling.

Prayer Time

Gratitiude— Begin your time of prayer by writing at least three things you are thankful for today. Cultivating a spirit of gratitude is such an important part of getting your day off to a good start.

Confession— I John 1:9 says, *"If we confess our sin, He is faithful and just to forgive us our sin and to cleanse us from all unrighteousness."* The best way to keep clear communication between us and God is through a clean heart. In Psalms 66:18, the psalmist writes, *"If I regard iniquity in my heart, the Lord will not hear me:"* Asking God to search our heart and reveal areas we have sinned against Him or others

Today's Day/Date: _____ / _____

Prayer Time

Gratitude: What three things am I grateful for today?
_____
_____
_____

Confession: What sins do I need to confess?
_____
_____
_____

Requests: What am I praying for today?
_____
_____
_____

Bible Reading

Reading:
_____

Journaling Thoughts:
_____
_____
_____
_____
_____
_____
_____
_____
_____
_____

My Tasks:
_____ _____ _____
_____ _____ _____
_____ _____ _____

will help to clear the guilty feelings we have and set us in a position to hear from God.

Sometimes I keep my confession general, such as, "forgive me from my attitude" or "I was really hurtful toward a friend." If I want to get specific, I use my own *short-hand*, so I know what it is but if someone picked up my journal they wouldn't be able to see all my "dirty laundry." That way I can truly confess my sin without hurting someone else's reputation and without being paranoid about my confession to God.

Requests— Before you begin to write, stop and ask God what you should ask for. James 4:3 clarifies why we struggle in this area of prayer, *"Ye ask, and receive not, because ye ask amiss, that ye may consume it upon your lusts."* Pray, "Lord, what do I need from You today that will help me to be more like You?" Pause and see what God lays on your heart to pray about or who to pray for.

Bible Reading Time

Bible Reading— Choose a Bible reading plan that works best for you. Be sure to have a pen to mark verses in your Bible that impact your heart. Underline, circle, and make notes in the margins for future reference so you can easily find and recall passages of the Bible that really encourage your heart. Record in your Faithfully Stepping Journal the passage or passages you have read for the day and write down your observations. I would also have a dictionary handy to define any words that you may not understand. Words have meanings. Specific words used in specific ways have very powerful meaning. There may be a word you know and are familiar with, but I would encourage you to look up the definition, write the word and definition in your journal and see how it fits with the truth the verse is communicating. By simply defining words, you will transform your Bible reading and take it to a whole new level. At the end of this guide, I have included several Bible reading plans.

Journaling Thoughts— Write down any thoughts or verses that jump out at you. You are just writing down what impacts you as you read. You will be amazed at the number of times the Holy Spirit will bring to mind what you read, and it will help guide your decisions and handling your emotions throughout the day.

Tasks— When I sit down to journal, inevitably tasks come to mind that I need to accomplish for the day. Thoughts of errands to run, groceries I need to add to my list, and more come to my mind right then. To help cut down on the distractions, I write down whatever thoughts come to mind. By doing this, I don't worry about forgetting the task and can quickly get back to what I was focused on at the moment--my time with God.

Bible Reading Ideas

1. Read a Proverb each day which corresponds with the date. For example: September 21—read Proverbs 21.

2. Read one Psalm each day.

3. Do a book study. Choose one book of the Bible. Read one chapter a day.

4. Do a character study. Study the life of a Bible character in detail.

5. Do a topical study. Maybe you want to have more peace in your life. Each day, look up verses containing the word peace. Write down the ones that impact you the most.

6. Buy a Bible study book and write down your application in this Journal.

7. Find a Bible Reading plan that will take you through the Bible in a year.

I pray that this journal will be a great encouragement to you and a tool to use to strengthen your walk with God. The truths you discover each day will become so precious and valuable to you that you will grow, mature, and find yourself transformed day after day. You will have encouragement to give to others, advice to help in times of need, and most of all a faith and hope that will set your course, not just for the day, but for the rest of your life.

God Bless,
Amanda Manney
November 2022

Today's Day/Date: _____ / _____

Prayer Time

Gratitude: What three things am I grateful for today?
_____
_____
_____

Confession: What sins do I need to confess?
_____
_____
_____

Requests: What am I praying for today?
_____
_____
_____

Bible Reading

Reading:
_____

Journaling Thoughts:
_____
_____
_____
_____
_____
_____
_____
_____
_____
_____
_____

My Tasks:

_____ _____ _____

_____ _____ _____

_____ _____ _____

Today's Day/Date: _____ / _____

Prayer Time

Gratitude: What three things am I grateful for today?
_____
_____
_____

Confession: What sins do I need to confess?
_____
_____
_____

Requests: What am I praying for today?
_____
_____
_____

Bible Reading

Reading:
_____

Journaling Thoughts:
_____
_____
_____
_____
_____
_____
_____
_____
_____
_____
_____

My Tasks:

_____	_____	_____
_____	_____	_____
_____	_____	_____

Today's Day/Date: _____ / _____

Prayer Time

Gratitude: What three things am I grateful for today?
_____
_____
_____

Confession: What sins do I need to confess?
_____
_____
_____

Requests: What am I praying for today?
_____
_____
_____

Bible Reading

Reading:
_____

Journaling Thoughts:
_____
_____
_____
_____
_____
_____
_____
_____
_____

My Tasks:

_____   _____   _____

_____   _____   _____

_____   _____   _____

Today's Day/Date: _____ / _____

Prayer Time

Gratitude: What three things am I grateful for today?
_____
_____
_____

Confession: What sins do I need to confess?
_____
_____
_____

Requests: What am I praying for today?
_____
_____
_____

Bible Reading

Reading:
_____

Journaling Thoughts:
_____
_____
_____
_____
_____
_____
_____
_____
_____
_____

My Tasks:

_____   _____   _____

_____   _____   _____

_____   _____   _____

Today's Day/Date: _____ / _____

Prayer Time

Gratitude: What three things am I grateful for today?
_____
_____
_____

Confession: What sins do I need to confess?
_____
_____
_____

Requests: What am I praying for today?
_____
_____
_____

Bible Reading

Reading:
_____

Journaling Thoughts:
_____
_____
_____
_____
_____
_____
_____
_____
_____
_____

My Tasks:

_____	_____	_____
_____	_____	_____
_____	_____	_____

Today's Day/Date: _____ / _____

Prayer Time

Gratitude: What three things am I grateful for today?
_____
_____
_____

Confession: What sins do I need to confess?
_____
_____
_____

Requests: What am I praying for today?
_____
_____
_____

Bible Reading

Reading:
_____

Journaling Thoughts:
_____
_____
_____
_____
_____
_____
_____
_____
_____
_____

My Tasks:

_____ _____ _____

_____ _____ _____

_____ _____ _____

Today's Day/Date: _____ / _____

Prayer Time

Gratitude: What three things am I grateful for today?
_____
_____
_____

Confession: What sins do I need to confess?
_____
_____
_____

Requests: What am I praying for today?
_____
_____
_____

Bible Reading

Reading:
_____

Journaling Thoughts:
_____
_____
_____
_____
_____
_____
_____
_____
_____
_____
_____

My Tasks:
_____ _____ _____
_____ _____ _____
_____ _____ _____

Today's Day/Date: _____ / _____

Prayer Time

Gratitude: What three things am I grateful for today?
_____
_____
_____

Confession: What sins do I need to confess?
_____
_____
_____

Requests: What am I praying for today?
_____
_____
_____

Bible Reading

Reading:
_____

Journaling Thoughts:
_____
_____
_____
_____
_____
_____
_____
_____
_____
_____

My Tasks:
_____ _____ _____

_____ _____ _____

_____ _____ _____

Today's Day/Date: _____ / _____

Prayer Time

Gratitude: What three things am I grateful for today?
_____
_____
_____

Confession: What sins do I need to confess?
_____
_____
_____

Requests: What am I praying for today?
_____
_____
_____

Bible Reading

Reading:
_____

Journaling Thoughts:
_____
_____
_____
_____
_____
_____
_____
_____
_____
_____

My Tasks:
_____ _____ _____

_____ _____ _____

_____ _____ _____

Today's Day/Date: _____ / _____

Prayer Time

Gratitude: What three things am I grateful for today?
_____
_____
_____

Confession: What sins do I need to confess?
_____
_____
_____

Requests: What am I praying for today?
_____
_____
_____

Bible Reading

Reading:
_____

Journaling Thoughts:
_____
_____
_____
_____
_____
_____
_____
_____
_____
_____

My Tasks:

_____ _____ _____

_____ _____ _____

_____ _____ _____

Today's Day/Date: _____ / _____

Prayer Time

Gratitude: What three things am I grateful for today?
_____
_____
_____

Confession: What sins do I need to confess?
_____
_____
_____

Requests: What am I praying for today?
_____
_____
_____

Bible Reading

Reading:
_____

Journaling Thoughts:
_____
_____
_____
_____
_____
_____
_____
_____
_____
_____
_____

My Tasks:
_____ _____ _____

_____ _____ _____

_____ _____ _____

Today's Day/Date: _____ / _____

Prayer Time

Gratitude: What three things am I grateful for today?
_____
_____
_____

Confession: What sins do I need to confess?
_____
_____
_____

Requests: What am I praying for today?
_____
_____
_____

Bible Reading

Reading:
_____

Journaling Thoughts:
_____
_____
_____
_____
_____
_____
_____
_____
_____
_____

My Tasks:

_____	_____	_____
_____	_____	_____
_____	_____	_____

Today's Day/Date: _____ / _____

Prayer Time

Gratitude: What three things am I grateful for today?
_____
_____
_____

Confession: What sins do I need to confess?
_____
_____
_____

Requests: What am I praying for today?
_____
_____
_____

Bible Reading

Reading:
_____

Journaling Thoughts:
_____
_____
_____
_____
_____
_____
_____
_____
_____
_____

My Tasks:

_____	_____	_____
_____	_____	_____
_____	_____	_____

Today's Day/Date: _____ / _____

Prayer Time

Gratitude: What three things am I grateful for today?
_____
_____
_____

Confession: What sins do I need to confess?
_____
_____
_____

Requests: What am I praying for today?
_____
_____
_____

Bible Reading

Reading:
_____

Journaling Thoughts:
_____
_____
_____
_____
_____
_____
_____
_____
_____
_____

My Tasks:

_____   _____   _____

_____   _____   _____

_____   _____   _____

Today's Day/Date: _____ / _____

Prayer Time

Gratitude: What three things am I grateful for today?
_____
_____
_____

Confession: What sins do I need to confess?
_____
_____
_____

Requests: What am I praying for today?
_____
_____
_____

Bible Reading

Reading:
_____

Journaling Thoughts:
_____
_____
_____
_____
_____
_____
_____
_____
_____
_____

My Tasks:
_____ _____ _____

_____ _____ _____

_____ _____ _____

Today's Day/Date: _____ / _____

Prayer Time

Gratitude: What three things am I grateful for today?
_____
_____
_____

Confession: What sins do I need to confess?
_____
_____
_____

Requests: What am I praying for today?
_____
_____
_____

Bible Reading

Reading:
_____

Journaling Thoughts:
_____
_____
_____
_____
_____
_____
_____
_____
_____
_____

My Tasks:
_____   _____   _____
_____   _____   _____
_____   _____   _____

Today's Day/Date: _____ / _____

Prayer Time

Gratitude: What three things am I grateful for today?
_____
_____
_____

Confession: What sins do I need to confess?
_____
_____
_____

Requests: What am I praying for today?
_____
_____
_____

Bible Reading

Reading:
_____

Journaling Thoughts:
_____
_____
_____
_____
_____
_____
_____
_____
_____
_____
_____

My Tasks:

_____	_____	_____
_____	_____	_____
_____	_____	_____

Today's Day/Date: _____ / _____

Prayer Time

Gratitude: What three things am I grateful for today?
_____
_____
_____

Confession: What sins do I need to confess?
_____
_____
_____

Requests: What am I praying for today?
_____
_____
_____

Bible Reading

Reading:
_____

Journaling Thoughts:
_____
_____
_____
_____
_____
_____
_____
_____
_____
_____

My Tasks:
- _____ _____ _____
- _____ _____ _____

Today's Day/Date: _____ / _____

Prayer Time

Gratitude: What three things am I grateful for today?
_____
_____
_____

Confession: What sins do I need to confess?
_____
_____
_____

Requests: What am I praying for today?
_____
_____
_____

Bible Reading

Reading:
_____

Journaling Thoughts:
_____
_____
_____
_____
_____
_____
_____
_____
_____
_____

My Tasks:

_____	_____	_____
_____	_____	_____
_____	_____	_____

Today's Day/Date: _____ / _____

Prayer Time

Gratitude: What three things am I grateful for today?
_____
_____
_____

Confession: What sins do I need to confess?
_____
_____
_____

Requests: What am I praying for today?
_____
_____
_____

Bible Reading

Reading:
_____

Journaling Thoughts:
_____
_____
_____
_____
_____
_____
_____
_____
_____
_____

My Tasks:

_____	_____	_____
_____	_____	_____
_____	_____	_____

Today's Day/Date: _____ / _____

Prayer Time

Gratitude: What three things am I grateful for today?
_____
_____
_____

Confession: What sins do I need to confess?
_____
_____
_____

Requests: What am I praying for today?
_____
_____
_____

Bible Reading

Reading:
_____

Journaling Thoughts:
_____
_____
_____
_____
_____
_____
_____
_____
_____
_____

My Tasks:
_____	_____	_____
_____	_____	_____
_____	_____	_____

Today's Day/Date: _____ / _____

Prayer Time

Gratitude: What three things am I grateful for today?
_____
_____
_____

Confession: What sins do I need to confess?
_____
_____
_____

Requests: What am I praying for today?
_____
_____
_____

Bible Reading

Reading:
_____

Journaling Thoughts:
_____
_____
_____
_____
_____
_____
_____
_____
_____
_____
_____

My Tasks:

_____	_____	_____
_____	_____	_____
_____	_____	_____

Today's Day/Date: _____ / _____

Prayer Time

Gratitude: What three things am I grateful for today?
_____
_____
_____

Confession: What sins do I need to confess?
_____
_____
_____

Requests: What am I praying for today?
_____
_____
_____

Bible Reading

Reading:
_____

Journaling Thoughts:
_____
_____
_____
_____
_____
_____
_____
_____
_____
_____

My Tasks:

_____ _____ _____

_____ _____ _____

Today's Day/Date: _____ / _____

Prayer Time

Gratitude: What three things am I grateful for today?
_____
_____
_____

Confession: What sins do I need to confess?
_____
_____
_____

Requests: What am I praying for today?
_____
_____
_____

Bible Reading

Reading:
_____

Journaling Thoughts:
_____
_____
_____
_____
_____
_____
_____
_____
_____
_____

My Tasks:

_____ _____ _____

_____ _____ _____

_____ _____ _____

Today's Day/Date: _____ / _____

Prayer Time

Gratitude: What three things am I grateful for today?
_____
_____
_____

Confession: What sins do I need to confess?
_____
_____
_____

Requests: What am I praying for today?
_____
_____
_____

Bible Reading

Reading:
_____

Journaling Thoughts:
_____
_____
_____
_____
_____
_____
_____
_____
_____
_____
_____

My Tasks:
_____ _____ _____

_____ _____ _____

_____ _____ _____

Today's Day/Date: _____ / _____

Prayer Time

Gratitude: What three things am I grateful for today?
_____
_____
_____

Confession: What sins do I need to confess?
_____
_____
_____

Requests: What am I praying for today?
_____
_____
_____

Bible Reading

Reading:
_____

Journaling Thoughts:
_____
_____
_____
_____
_____
_____
_____
_____
_____
_____

My Tasks:
_____ _____ _____

_____ _____ _____

_____ _____ _____

Today's Day / Date: _____ / _____

Prayer Time

Gratitude: What three things am I grateful for today?
_____
_____
_____

Confession: What sins do I need to confess?
_____
_____
_____

Requests: What am I praying for today?
_____
_____
_____

Bible Reading

Reading:
_____

Journaling Thoughts:
_____
_____
_____
_____
_____
_____
_____
_____
_____
_____

My Tasks:
_____	_____	_____
_____	_____	_____
_____	_____	_____

Today's Day / Date: _____ / _____

Prayer Time

Gratitude: What three things am I grateful for today?
_____
_____
_____

Confession: What sins do I need to confess?
_____
_____
_____

Requests: What am I praying for today?
_____
_____
_____

Bible Reading

Reading:
_____

Journaling Thoughts:
_____
_____
_____
_____
_____
_____
_____
_____
_____
_____

My Tasks:
_____ _____ _____
_____ _____ _____
_____ _____ _____

Today's Day/Date: _____ / _____

Prayer Time

Gratitude: What three things am I grateful for today?
_____
_____
_____

Confession: What sins do I need to confess?
_____
_____
_____

Requests: What am I praying for today?
_____
_____
_____

Bible Reading

Reading:
_____

Journaling Thoughts:
_____
_____
_____
_____
_____
_____
_____
_____
_____
_____

My Tasks:

_____	_____	_____
_____	_____	_____
_____	_____	_____

Today's Day/Date: _____ / _____

Prayer Time

Gratitude: What three things am I grateful for today?
_____
_____
_____

Confession: What sins do I need to confess?
_____
_____
_____

Requests: What am I praying for today?
_____
_____
_____

Bible Reading

Reading:
_____

Journaling Thoughts:
_____
_____
_____
_____
_____
_____
_____
_____
_____
_____

My Tasks:

_____	_____	_____
_____	_____	_____
_____	_____	_____

Today's Day/Date: _____ / _____

Prayer Time

Gratitude: What three things am I grateful for today?
_____
_____
_____

Confession: What sins do I need to confess?
_____
_____
_____

Requests: What am I praying for today?
_____
_____
_____

Bible Reading

Reading:
_____

Journaling Thoughts:
_____
_____
_____
_____
_____
_____
_____
_____
_____
_____

My Tasks:

_____ _____ _____

_____ _____ _____

Today's Day / Date: _____ / _____

Prayer Time

Gratitude: What three things am I grateful for today?
_____
_____
_____

Confession: What sins do I need to confess?
_____
_____
_____

Requests: What am I praying for today?
_____
_____
_____

Bible Reading

Reading:
_____

Journaling Thoughts:
_____
_____
_____
_____
_____
_____
_____
_____
_____
_____

My Tasks:

_____	_____	_____
_____	_____	_____
_____	_____	_____

Today's Day/Date: _____ / _____

Prayer Time

Gratitude: What three things am I grateful for today?
_____
_____
_____

Confession: What sins do I need to confess?
_____
_____
_____

Requests: What am I praying for today?
_____
_____
_____

Bible Reading

Reading:
_____

Journaling Thoughts:
_____
_____
_____
_____
_____
_____
_____
_____
_____
_____

My Tasks:
_____	_____	_____
_____	_____	_____
_____	_____	_____

Today's Day/Date: _____ / _____

Prayer Time

Gratitude: What three things am I grateful for today?
_____
_____
_____

Confession: What sins do I need to confess?
_____
_____
_____

Requests: What am I praying for today?
_____
_____
_____

Bible Reading

Reading:
_____

Journaling Thoughts:
_____
_____
_____
_____
_____
_____
_____
_____
_____

My Tasks:
_____	_____	_____
_____	_____	_____
_____	_____	_____

Today's Day/Date: _____ / _____

Prayer Time

Gratitude: What three things am I grateful for today?
_____
_____
_____

Confession: What sins do I need to confess?
_____
_____
_____

Requests: What am I praying for today?
_____
_____
_____

Bible Reading

Reading:
_____

Journaling Thoughts:
_____
_____
_____
_____
_____
_____
_____
_____
_____
_____

My Tasks:
_____   _____   _____
_____   _____   _____
_____   _____   _____

Today's Day/Date: _____ / _____

Prayer Time

Gratitude: What three things am I grateful for today?
_____
_____
_____

Confession: What sins do I need to confess?
_____
_____
_____

Requests: What am I praying for today?
_____
_____
_____

Bible Reading

Reading:
_____

Journaling Thoughts:
_____
_____
_____
_____
_____
_____
_____
_____
_____
_____
_____
_____

My Tasks:

_____	_____	_____
_____	_____	_____
_____	_____	_____

Today's Day/Date: _____ / _____

Prayer Time

Gratitude: What three things am I grateful for today?
_____
_____
_____

Confession: What sins do I need to confess?
_____
_____
_____

Requests: What am I praying for today?
_____
_____
_____

Bible Reading

Reading:
_____

Journaling Thoughts:
_____
_____
_____
_____
_____
_____
_____
_____
_____
_____

My Tasks:

_____ _____ _____

_____ _____ _____

Today's Day/Date: _____ / _____

Prayer Time

Gratitude: What three things am I grateful for today?
_____
_____
_____

Confession: What sins do I need to confess?
_____
_____
_____

Requests: What am I praying for today?
_____
_____
_____

Bible Reading

Reading:
_____

Journaling Thoughts:
_____
_____
_____
_____
_____
_____
_____
_____
_____
_____

My Tasks:

_____	_____	_____
_____	_____	_____
_____	_____	_____

Today's Day/Date: _____ / _____

Prayer Time

Gratitude: What three things am I grateful for today?
_____
_____
_____

Confession: What sins do I need to confess?
_____
_____
_____

Requests: What am I praying for today?
_____
_____
_____

Bible Reading

Reading:
_____

Journaling Thoughts:
_____
_____
_____
_____
_____
_____
_____
_____
_____
_____

My Tasks:

_____	_____	_____
_____	_____	_____
_____	_____	_____

Today's Day/Date: _____ / _____

Prayer Time

Gratitude: What three things am I grateful for today?
_____
_____
_____

Confession: What sins do I need to confess?
_____
_____
_____

Requests: What am I praying for today?
_____
_____
_____

Bible Reading

Reading:
_____

Journaling Thoughts:
_____
_____
_____
_____
_____
_____
_____
_____
_____
_____
_____

My Tasks:

_____	_____	_____
_____	_____	_____
_____	_____	_____

Today's Day/Date: _____ / _____

Prayer Time

Gratitude: What three things am I grateful for today?
_____
_____
_____

Confession: What sins do I need to confess?
_____
_____
_____

Requests: What am I praying for today?
_____
_____
_____

Bible Reading

Reading:
_____

Journaling Thoughts:
_____
_____
_____
_____
_____
_____
_____
_____
_____
_____
_____

My Tasks:
_____   _____   _____
_____   _____   _____
_____   _____   _____

Today's Day/Date: _____ / _____

Prayer Time

Gratitude: What three things am I grateful for today?
_____
_____
_____

Confession: What sins do I need to confess?
_____
_____
_____

Requests: What am I praying for today?
_____
_____
_____

Bible Reading

Reading:
_____

Journaling Thoughts:
_____
_____
_____
_____
_____
_____
_____
_____
_____
_____
_____

My Tasks:
_____ _____ _____
_____ _____ _____
_____ _____ _____

Today's Day/Date: _____ / _____

Prayer Time

Gratitude: What three things am I grateful for today?
_____
_____
_____

Confession: What sins do I need to confess?
_____
_____
_____

Requests: What am I praying for today?
_____
_____
_____

Bible Reading

Reading:
_____

Journaling Thoughts:
_____
_____
_____
_____
_____
_____
_____
_____
_____
_____
_____

My Tasks:

_____	_____	_____
_____	_____	_____
_____	_____	_____

Today's Day/Date: _____ / _____

Prayer Time

Gratitude: What three things am I grateful for today?
_____
_____
_____

Confession: What sins do I need to confess?
_____
_____
_____

Requests: What am I praying for today?
_____
_____
_____

Bible Reading

Reading:
_____

Journaling Thoughts:
_____
_____
_____
_____
_____
_____
_____
_____
_____
_____

My Tasks:
| _____ | _____ | _____ |
| _____ | _____ | _____ |

Today's Day/Date: _____ / _____

Prayer Time

Gratitude: What three things am I grateful for today?
_____
_____
_____

Confession: What sins do I need to confess?
_____
_____
_____

Requests: What am I praying for today?
_____
_____
_____

Bible Reading

Reading:
_____

Journaling Thoughts:
_____
_____
_____
_____
_____
_____
_____
_____
_____
_____

My Tasks:

_____   _____   _____

_____   _____   _____

_____   _____   _____

Today's Day/Date: _____ / _____

Prayer Time

Gratitude: What three things am I grateful for today?
_____
_____
_____

Confession: What sins do I need to confess?
_____
_____
_____

Requests: What am I praying for today?
_____
_____
_____

Bible Reading

Reading:
_____

Journaling Thoughts:
_____
_____
_____
_____
_____
_____
_____
_____
_____
_____

My Tasks:
_____   _____   _____

_____   _____   _____

_____   _____   _____

Today's Day/Date: _____ / _____

Prayer Time

Gratitude: What three things am I grateful for today?
_____
_____
_____

Confession: What sins do I need to confess?
_____
_____
_____

Requests: What am I praying for today?
_____
_____
_____

Bible Reading

Reading:
_____

Journaling Thoughts:
_____
_____
_____
_____
_____
_____
_____
_____
_____
_____

My Tasks:

_____   _____   _____

_____   _____   _____

_____   _____   _____

Today's Day/Date: _____ / _____

Prayer Time

Gratitude: What three things am I grateful for today?
_____
_____
_____

Confession: What sins do I need to confess?
_____
_____
_____

Requests: What am I praying for today?
_____
_____
_____

Bible Reading

Reading:
_____

Journaling Thoughts:
_____
_____
_____
_____
_____
_____
_____
_____
_____
_____

My Tasks:

_____   _____   _____

_____   _____   _____

_____   _____   _____

Today's Day/Date: _____ / _____

Prayer Time

Gratitude: What three things am I grateful for today?
_____
_____
_____

Confession: What sins do I need to confess?
_____
_____
_____

Requests: What am I praying for today?
_____
_____
_____

Bible Reading

Reading:
_____

Journaling Thoughts:
_____
_____
_____
_____
_____
_____
_____
_____
_____
_____

My Tasks:

_____ _____ _____

_____ _____ _____

_____ _____

Today's Day/Date: _____ / _____

Prayer Time

Gratitude: What three things am I grateful for today?
_____
_____
_____

Confession: What sins do I need to confess?
_____
_____
_____

Requests: What am I praying for today?
_____
_____
_____

Bible Reading

Reading:
_____

Journaling Thoughts:
_____
_____
_____
_____
_____
_____
_____
_____
_____
_____

My Tasks:

_____	_____	_____
_____	_____	_____
_____	_____	_____

Today's Day/Date: _____ / _____

Prayer Time

Gratitude: What three things am I grateful for today?
_____
_____
_____

Confession: What sins do I need to confess?
_____
_____
_____

Requests: What am I praying for today?
_____
_____
_____

Bible Reading

Reading:
_____

Journaling Thoughts:
_____
_____
_____
_____
_____
_____
_____
_____
_____
_____

My Tasks:

_____	_____	_____
_____	_____	_____
_____	_____	_____

Today's Day/Date: _____ / _____

Prayer Time

Gratitude: What three things am I grateful for today?
_____
_____
_____

Confession: What sins do I need to confess?
_____
_____
_____

Requests: What am I praying for today?
_____
_____
_____

Bible Reading

Reading:
_____

Journaling Thoughts:
_____
_____
_____
_____
_____
_____
_____
_____
_____
_____

My Tasks:

_____	_____	_____
_____	_____	_____
_____	_____	_____

Today's Day/Date: _____ / _____

Prayer Time

Gratitude: What three things am I grateful for today?
_____
_____
_____

Confession: What sins do I need to confess?
_____
_____
_____

Requests: What am I praying for today?
_____
_____
_____

Bible Reading

Reading:
_____

Journaling Thoughts:
_____
_____
_____
_____
_____
_____
_____
_____
_____
_____

My Tasks:

_____	_____	_____
_____	_____	_____
_____	_____	_____

Today's Day/Date: _____ / _____

Prayer Time

Gratitude: What three things am I grateful for today?
_____
_____
_____

Confession: What sins do I need to confess?
_____
_____
_____

Requests: What am I praying for today?
_____
_____
_____

Bible Reading

Reading:
_____

Journaling Thoughts:
_____
_____
_____
_____
_____
_____
_____
_____
_____
_____

My Tasks:

_____	_____	_____
_____	_____	_____
_____	_____	_____

Today's Day/Date: _____ / _____

Prayer Time

Gratitude: What three things am I grateful for today?
_____
_____
_____

Confession: What sins do I need to confess?
_____
_____
_____

Requests: What am I praying for today?
_____
_____
_____

Bible Reading

Reading:
_____

Journaling Thoughts:
_____
_____
_____
_____
_____
_____
_____
_____
_____
_____

My Tasks:
_____ _____ _____

_____ _____ _____

_____ _____ _____

Today's Day/Date: _____ / _____

Prayer Time

Gratitude: What three things am I grateful for today?
_____
_____
_____

Confession: What sins do I need to confess?
_____
_____
_____

Requests: What am I praying for today?
_____
_____
_____

Bible Reading

Reading:
_____

Journaling Thoughts:
_____
_____
_____
_____
_____
_____
_____
_____
_____
_____

My Tasks:
_____ _____ _____

_____ _____ _____

_____ _____ _____

Today's Day/Date: _____ / _____

Prayer Time

Gratitude: What three things am I grateful for today?
_____
_____
_____

Confession: What sins do I need to confess?
_____
_____
_____

Requests: What am I praying for today?
_____
_____
_____

Bible Reading

Reading:
_____

Journaling Thoughts:
_____
_____
_____
_____
_____
_____
_____
_____
_____
_____

My Tasks:

_____ _____ _____

_____ _____ _____

_____ _____ _____

Today's Day/Date: _____ / _____

Prayer Time

Gratitude: What three things am I grateful for today?
_____
_____
_____

Confession: What sins do I need to confess?
_____
_____
_____

Requests: What am I praying for today?
_____
_____
_____

Bible Reading

Reading:
_____

Journaling Thoughts:
_____
_____
_____
_____
_____
_____
_____
_____
_____
_____

My Tasks:

_____ _____ _____ _____

_____ _____ _____ _____

_____ _____ _____ _____

Today's Day/Date: _____ / _____

Prayer Time

Gratitude: What three things am I grateful for today?
_____
_____
_____

Confession: What sins do I need to confess?
_____
_____
_____

Requests: What am I praying for today?
_____
_____
_____

Bible Reading

Reading:
_____

Journaling Thoughts:
_____
_____
_____
_____
_____
_____
_____
_____
_____
_____

My Tasks:
_____	_____	_____
_____	_____	_____
_____	_____	_____

Today's Day/Date: _____ / _____

Prayer Time

Gratitude: What three things am I grateful for today?
_____
_____
_____

Confession: What sins do I need to confess?
_____
_____
_____

Requests: What am I praying for today?
_____
_____
_____

Bible Reading

Reading:
_____

Journaling Thoughts:
_____
_____
_____
_____
_____
_____
_____
_____
_____
_____

My Tasks:
_____ _____ _____
_____ _____ _____
_____ _____ _____

Today's Day/Date: _____ / _____

Prayer Time

Gratitude: What three things am I grateful for today?
_____
_____
_____

Confession: What sins do I need to confess?
_____
_____
_____

Requests: What am I praying for today?
_____
_____
_____

Bible Reading

Reading:
_____

Journaling Thoughts:
_____
_____
_____
_____
_____
_____
_____
_____
_____
_____

My Tasks:
_____ _____ _____
_____ _____ _____
_____ _____ _____

Today's Day/Date: _____ / _____

Prayer Time

Gratitude: What three things am I grateful for today?
_____
_____
_____

Confession: What sins do I need to confess?
_____
_____
_____

Requests: What am I praying for today?
_____
_____
_____

Bible Reading

Reading:
_____

Journaling Thoughts:
_____
_____
_____
_____
_____
_____
_____
_____
_____
_____

My Tasks:
_____ _____ _____
_____ _____ _____
_____ _____ _____

Today's Day/Date: _____ / _____

Prayer Time

Gratitude: What three things am I grateful for today?
_____
_____
_____

Confession: What sins do I need to confess?
_____
_____
_____

Requests: What am I praying for today?
_____
_____
_____

Bible Reading

Reading:
_____

Journaling Thoughts:
_____
_____
_____
_____
_____
_____
_____
_____
_____
_____
_____

My Tasks:

_____	_____	_____
_____	_____	_____
_____	_____	_____

Today's Day/Date: _____ / _____

Prayer Time

Gratitude: What three things am I grateful for today?
_____
_____
_____

Confession: What sins do I need to confess?
_____
_____
_____

Requests: What am I praying for today?
_____
_____
_____

Bible Reading

Reading:
_____

Journaling Thoughts:
_____
_____
_____
_____
_____
_____
_____
_____
_____
_____

My Tasks:

_____	_____	_____
_____	_____	_____
_____	_____	_____

Today's Day/Date: _____ / _____

Prayer Time

Gratitude: What three things am I grateful for today?
_____
_____
_____

Confession: What sins do I need to confess?
_____
_____
_____

Requests: What am I praying for today?
_____
_____
_____

Bible Reading

Reading:
_____

Journaling Thoughts:
_____
_____
_____
_____
_____
_____
_____
_____
_____
_____

My Tasks:
_____ _____ _____

_____ _____ _____

_____ _____ _____

Today's Day/Date: _____ / _____

Prayer Time

Gratitude: What three things am I grateful for today?
_____
_____
_____

Confession: What sins do I need to confess?
_____
_____
_____

Requests: What am I praying for today?
_____
_____
_____

Bible Reading

Reading:
_____

Journaling Thoughts:
_____
_____
_____
_____
_____
_____
_____
_____
_____
_____

My Tasks:
_____ _____ _____

_____ _____ _____

Today's Day/Date: _____ / _____

Prayer Time

Gratitude: What three things am I grateful for today?
_____
_____
_____

Confession: What sins do I need to confess?
_____
_____
_____

Requests: What am I praying for today?
_____
_____
_____

Bible Reading

Reading:
_____

Journaling Thoughts:
_____
_____
_____
_____
_____
_____
_____
_____
_____
_____

My Tasks:
_____ _____ _____
_____ _____ _____
_____ _____ _____

Today's Day/Date: _____ / _____

Prayer Time

Gratitude: What three things am I grateful for today?
_____
_____
_____

Confession: What sins do I need to confess?
_____
_____
_____

Requests: What am I praying for today?
_____
_____
_____

Bible Reading

Reading:
_____

Journaling Thoughts:
_____
_____
_____
_____
_____
_____
_____
_____
_____
_____

My Tasks:

_____	_____	_____
_____	_____	_____
_____	_____	_____

Today's Day/Date: _____ / _____

Prayer Time

Gratitude: What three things am I grateful for today?
_____
_____
_____

Confession: What sins do I need to confess?
_____
_____
_____

Requests: What am I praying for today?
_____
_____
_____

Bible Reading

Reading:
_____

Journaling Thoughts:
_____
_____
_____
_____
_____
_____
_____
_____
_____
_____
_____

My Tasks:

_____   _____   _____

_____   _____   _____

_____   _____   _____

Today's Day/Date: _____ / _____

Prayer Time

Gratitude: What three things am I grateful for today?
_____
_____
_____

Confession: What sins do I need to confess?
_____
_____
_____

Requests: What am I praying for today?
_____
_____
_____

Bible Reading

Reading:
_____

Journaling Thoughts:
_____
_____
_____
_____
_____
_____
_____
_____
_____
_____

My Tasks:
_____	_____	_____
_____	_____	_____
_____	_____	_____

Today's Day/Date: _____ / _____

Prayer Time

Gratitude: What three things am I grateful for today?
_____
_____
_____

Confession: What sins do I need to confess?
_____
_____
_____

Requests: What am I praying for today?
_____
_____
_____

Bible Reading

Reading:
_____

Journaling Thoughts:
_____
_____
_____
_____
_____
_____
_____
_____
_____
_____
_____

My Tasks:

_____   _____   _____

_____   _____   _____

_____   _____   _____

Today's Day/Date: _____ / _____

Prayer Time

Gratitude: What three things am I grateful for today?
_____
_____
_____

Confession: What sins do I need to confess?
_____
_____
_____

Requests: What am I praying for today?
_____
_____
_____

Bible Reading

Reading:
_____

Journaling Thoughts:
_____
_____
_____
_____
_____
_____
_____
_____
_____
_____

My Tasks:

_____   _____   _____

_____   _____   _____

_____   _____   _____

Today's Day/Date: _____ / _____

Prayer Time

Gratitude: What three things am I grateful for today?
_____
_____
_____

Confession: What sins do I need to confess?
_____
_____
_____

Requests: What am I praying for today?
_____
_____
_____

Bible Reading

Reading:
_____

Journaling Thoughts:
_____
_____
_____
_____
_____
_____
_____
_____
_____
_____
_____

My Tasks:

_____	_____	_____
_____	_____	_____
_____	_____	_____

Today's Day/Date: _____ / _____

Prayer Time

Gratitude: What three things am I grateful for today?
_____
_____
_____

Confession: What sins do I need to confess?
_____
_____
_____

Requests: What am I praying for today?
_____
_____
_____

Bible Reading

Reading:
_____

Journaling Thoughts:
_____
_____
_____
_____
_____
_____
_____
_____
_____
_____

My Tasks:

| _____ | _____ | _____ |
| _____ | _____ | _____ |

Today's Day/Date: _____ / _____

Prayer Time

Gratitude: What three things am I grateful for today?
_____
_____
_____

Confession: What sins do I need to confess?
_____
_____
_____

Requests: What am I praying for today?
_____
_____
_____

Bible Reading

Reading:
_____

Journaling Thoughts:
_____
_____
_____
_____
_____
_____
_____
_____
_____
_____

My Tasks:

_____	_____	_____
_____	_____	_____
_____	_____	_____

Today's Day/Date: _____ / _____

Prayer Time

Gratitude: What three things am I grateful for today?
_____
_____
_____

Confession: What sins do I need to confess?
_____
_____
_____

Requests: What am I praying for today?
_____
_____
_____

Bible Reading

Reading:
_____

Journaling Thoughts:
_____
_____
_____
_____
_____
_____
_____
_____
_____
_____

My Tasks:
_____   _____   _____

_____   _____   _____

_____   _____   _____

Today's Day/Date: _____ / _____

Prayer Time

Gratitude: What three things am I grateful for today?
_____
_____
_____

Confession: What sins do I need to confess?
_____
_____
_____

Requests: What am I praying for today?
_____
_____
_____

Bible Reading

Reading:
_____

Journaling Thoughts:
_____
_____
_____
_____
_____
_____
_____
_____
_____
_____

My Tasks:

_____ _____ _____

_____ _____ _____

_____ _____ _____

Today's Day/Date: _____ / _____

Prayer Time

Gratitude: What three things am I grateful for today?
_____
_____
_____

Confession: What sins do I need to confess?
_____
_____
_____

Requests: What am I praying for today?
_____
_____
_____

Bible Reading

Reading:
_____

Journaling Thoughts:
_____
_____
_____
_____
_____
_____
_____
_____
_____
_____

My Tasks:

_____	_____	_____
_____	_____	_____
_____	_____	_____

Today's Day/Date: _____ / _____

Prayer Time

Gratitude: What three things am I grateful for today?
_____
_____
_____

Confession: What sins do I need to confess?
_____
_____
_____

Requests: What am I praying for today?
_____
_____
_____

Bible Reading

Reading:
_____

Journaling Thoughts:
_____
_____
_____
_____
_____
_____
_____
_____
_____
_____

My Tasks:

Today's Day / Date: _____ / _____

Prayer Time

Gratitude: What three things am I grateful for today?
_____
_____
_____

Confession: What sins do I need to confess?
_____
_____
_____

Requests: What am I praying for today?
_____
_____
_____

Bible Reading

Reading:
_____

Journaling Thoughts:
_____
_____
_____
_____
_____
_____
_____
_____
_____
_____
_____
_____

My Tasks:
_____ _____ _____
_____ _____ _____
_____ _____ _____

Today's Day/Date: _____ / _____

Prayer Time

Gratitude: What three things am I grateful for today?
_____
_____
_____

Confession: What sins do I need to confess?
_____
_____
_____

Requests: What am I praying for today?
_____
_____
_____

Bible Reading

Reading:
_____

Journaling Thoughts:
_____
_____
_____
_____
_____
_____
_____
_____
_____
_____
_____

My Tasks:
_____ _____ _____
_____ _____ _____

Today's Day/Date: _____ / _____

Prayer Time

Gratitude: What three things am I grateful for today?
_____
_____
_____

Confession: What sins do I need to confess?
_____
_____
_____

Requests: What am I praying for today?
_____
_____
_____

Bible Reading

Reading:
_____

Journaling Thoughts:
_____
_____
_____
_____
_____
_____
_____
_____
_____
_____
_____

My Tasks:

_____	_____	_____
_____	_____	_____
_____	_____	_____

Today's Day / Date: _____ / _____

Prayer Time

Gratitude: What three things am I grateful for today?
_____
_____
_____

Confession: What sins do I need to confess?
_____
_____
_____

Requests: What am I praying for today?
_____
_____
_____

Bible Reading

Reading:
_____

Journaling Thoughts:
_____
_____
_____
_____
_____
_____
_____
_____
_____
_____

My Tasks:

_____   _____   _____

_____   _____   _____

_____   _____   _____

Today's Day/Date: _____ / _____

Prayer Time

Gratitude: What three things am I grateful for today?
_____
_____
_____

Confession: What sins do I need to confess?
_____
_____
_____

Requests: What am I praying for today?
_____
_____
_____

Bible Reading

Reading:
_____

Journaling Thoughts:
_____
_____
_____
_____
_____
_____
_____
_____
_____
_____

My Tasks:

_____   _____   _____

_____   _____   _____

Today's Day/Date: _____ / _____

Prayer Time

Gratitude: What three things am I grateful for today?
_____
_____
_____

Confession: What sins do I need to confess?
_____
_____
_____

Requests: What am I praying for today?
_____
_____
_____

Bible Reading

Reading:
_____

Journaling Thoughts:
_____
_____
_____
_____
_____
_____
_____
_____
_____
_____
_____

My Tasks:
_____ _____ _____

_____ _____ _____

_____ _____ _____

Today's Day/Date: _____ / _____

Prayer Time

Gratitude: What three things am I grateful for today?
_____
_____
_____

Confession: What sins do I need to confess?
_____
_____
_____

Requests: What am I praying for today?
_____
_____
_____

Bible Reading

Reading:
_____

Journaling Thoughts:
_____
_____
_____
_____
_____
_____
_____
_____
_____
_____

My Tasks:
_____ _____ _____
_____ _____ _____
_____ _____ _____

Today's Day/Date: _____ / _____

Prayer Time

Gratitude: What three things am I grateful for today?
_____
_____
_____

Confession: What sins do I need to confess?
_____
_____
_____

Requests: What am I praying for today?
_____
_____
_____

Bible Reading

Reading:
_____

Journaling Thoughts:
_____
_____
_____
_____
_____
_____
_____
_____
_____
_____

My Tasks:
_____ _____ _____
_____ _____ _____
_____ _____ _____

Today's Day/Date: _____ / _____

Prayer Time

Gratitude: What three things am I grateful for today?
_____
_____
_____

Confession: What sins do I need to confess?
_____
_____
_____

Requests: What am I praying for today?
_____
_____
_____

Bible Reading

Reading:
_____

Journaling Thoughts:
_____
_____
_____
_____
_____
_____
_____
_____
_____
_____

My Tasks:
- _____ _____ _____
- _____ _____ _____

Today's Day/Date: _____ / _____

Prayer Time

Gratitude: What three things am I grateful for today?
_____
_____
_____

Confession: What sins do I need to confess?
_____
_____
_____

Requests: What am I praying for today?
_____
_____
_____

Bible Reading

Reading:
_____

Journaling Thoughts:
_____
_____
_____
_____
_____
_____
_____
_____
_____
_____

My Tasks:
_____ _____ _____

_____ _____ _____

Today's Day/Date: _____ / _____

Prayer Time

Gratitude: What three things am I grateful for today?
_____
_____
_____

Confession: What sins do I need to confess?
_____
_____
_____

Requests: What am I praying for today?
_____
_____
_____

Bible Reading

Reading:
_____

Journaling Thoughts:
_____
_____
_____
_____
_____
_____
_____
_____
_____

My Tasks:

| _____ | _____ | _____ |
| _____ | _____ | _____ |

Today's Day/Date: _____ / _____

Prayer Time

Gratitude: What three things am I grateful for today?
_____
_____
_____

Confession: What sins do I need to confess?
_____
_____
_____

Requests: What am I praying for today?
_____
_____
_____

Bible Reading

Reading:
_____

Journaling Thoughts:
_____
_____
_____
_____
_____
_____
_____
_____
_____
_____

My Tasks:
_____ _____ _____
_____ _____ _____
_____ _____ _____

Today's Day / Date: _____ / _____

Prayer Time

Gratitude: What three things am I grateful for today?
_____
_____
_____

Confession: What sins do I need to confess?
_____
_____
_____

Requests: What am I praying for today?
_____
_____
_____

Bible Reading

Reading:
_____

Journaling Thoughts:
_____
_____
_____
_____
_____
_____
_____
_____
_____
_____

My Tasks:

_____	_____	_____
_____	_____	_____
_____	_____	_____

Today's Day/Date: _____ / _____

Prayer Time

Gratitude: What three things am I grateful for today?
_____
_____
_____

Confession: What sins do I need to confess?
_____
_____
_____

Requests: What am I praying for today?
_____
_____
_____

Bible Reading

Reading:
_____

Journaling Thoughts:
_____
_____
_____
_____
_____
_____
_____
_____
_____
_____
_____

My Tasks:

_____	_____	_____
_____	_____	_____
_____	_____	_____

Today's Day / Date: _____ / _____

Prayer Time

Gratitude: What three things am I grateful for today?
_____
_____
_____

Confession: What sins do I need to confess?
_____
_____
_____

Requests: What am I praying for today?
_____
_____
_____

Bible Reading

Reading:
_____

Journaling Thoughts:
_____
_____
_____
_____
_____
_____
_____
_____
_____
_____

My Tasks:

_____	_____	_____
_____	_____	_____
_____	_____	_____

Today's Day/Date: _____ / _____

Prayer Time

Gratitude: What three things am I grateful for today?
_____
_____
_____

Confession: What sins do I need to confess?
_____
_____
_____

Requests: What am I praying for today?
_____
_____
_____

Bible Reading

Reading:
_____

Journaling Thoughts:
_____
_____
_____
_____
_____
_____
_____
_____
_____
_____
_____

My Tasks:

_____ _____ _____

_____ _____ _____

_____ _____ _____

Today's Day/Date: _____ / _____

Prayer Time

Gratitude: What three things am I grateful for today?
_____
_____
_____

Confession: What sins do I need to confess?
_____
_____
_____

Requests: What am I praying for today?
_____
_____
_____

Bible Reading

Reading:
_____

Journaling Thoughts:
_____
_____
_____
_____
_____
_____
_____
_____
_____
_____

My Tasks:
_____ _____ _____
_____ _____ _____
_____ _____ _____

Today's Day/Date: _____ / _____

Prayer Time

Gratitude: What three things am I grateful for today?
_____
_____
_____

Confession: What sins do I need to confess?
_____
_____
_____

Requests: What am I praying for today?
_____
_____
_____

Bible Reading

Reading:
_____

Journaling Thoughts:
_____
_____
_____
_____
_____
_____
_____
_____
_____
_____
_____

My Tasks:
_____ _____ _____

_____ _____ _____

_____ _____ _____

Today's Day / Date: _____ / _____

Prayer Time

Gratitude: What three things am I grateful for today?
_____
_____
_____

Confession: What sins do I need to confess?
_____
_____
_____

Requests: What am I praying for today?
_____
_____
_____

Bible Reading

Reading:
_____

Journaling Thoughts:
_____
_____
_____
_____
_____
_____
_____
_____
_____
_____

My Tasks:

_____ _____ _____

_____ _____ _____

_____ _____ _____

Today's Day/Date: _____ / _____

Prayer Time

Gratitude: What three things am I grateful for today?
_____
_____
_____

Confession: What sins do I need to confess?
_____
_____
_____

Requests: What am I praying for today?
_____
_____
_____

Bible Reading

Reading:
_____

Journaling Thoughts:
_____
_____
_____
_____
_____
_____
_____
_____
_____
_____
_____

My Tasks:
_____ _____ _____
_____ _____ _____
_____ _____ _____

Today's Day / Date: _____ / _____

Prayer Time

Gratitude: What three things am I grateful for today?
_____
_____
_____

Confession: What sins do I need to confess?
_____
_____
_____

Requests: What am I praying for today?
_____
_____
_____

Bible Reading

Reading:
_____

Journaling Thoughts:
_____
_____
_____
_____
_____
_____
_____
_____
_____
_____

My Tasks:

Today's Day/Date: _____ / _____

Prayer Time

Gratitude: What three things am I grateful for today?
_____
_____
_____

Confession: What sins do I need to confess?
_____
_____
_____

Requests: What am I praying for today?
_____
_____
_____

Bible Reading

Reading:
_____

Journaling Thoughts:
_____
_____
_____
_____
_____
_____
_____
_____
_____
_____

My Tasks:
_____ _____ _____
_____ _____ _____
_____ _____ _____

Today's Day/Date: _____ / _____

Prayer Time

Gratitude: What three things am I grateful for today?
_____
_____
_____

Confession: What sins do I need to confess?
_____
_____
_____

Requests: What am I praying for today?
_____
_____
_____

Bible Reading

Reading:
_____

Journaling Thoughts:
_____
_____
_____
_____
_____
_____
_____
_____
_____
_____
_____

My Tasks:
_____ _____ _____
_____ _____ _____
_____ _____ _____

Today's Day/Date: _____ / _____

Prayer Time

Gratitude: What three things am I grateful for today?
_____
_____
_____

Confession: What sins do I need to confess?
_____
_____
_____

Requests: What am I praying for today?
_____
_____
_____

Bible Reading

Reading:
_____

Journaling Thoughts:
_____
_____
_____
_____
_____
_____
_____
_____
_____
_____

My Tasks:

_____	_____	_____
_____	_____	_____
_____	_____	_____

Today's Day/Date: _____ / _____

Prayer Time

Gratitude: What three things am I grateful for today?
_____
_____
_____

Confession: What sins do I need to confess?
_____
_____
_____

Requests: What am I praying for today?
_____
_____
_____

Bible Reading

Reading:
_____

Journaling Thoughts:
_____
_____
_____
_____
_____
_____
_____
_____
_____
_____

My Tasks:

_____ _____ _____

_____ _____ _____

_____ _____ _____

Today's Day/Date: _____ / _____

Prayer Time

Gratitude: What three things am I grateful for today?
_____
_____
_____

Confession: What sins do I need to confess?
_____
_____
_____

Requests: What am I praying for today?
_____
_____
_____

Bible Reading

Reading:
_____

Journaling Thoughts:
_____
_____
_____
_____
_____
_____
_____
_____
_____
_____
_____

My Tasks:
_____ _____ _____

_____ _____ _____

_____ _____ _____

Today's Day/Date: _____ / _____

Prayer Time

Gratitude: What three things am I grateful for today?
_____
_____
_____

Confession: What sins do I need to confess?
_____
_____
_____

Requests: What am I praying for today?
_____
_____
_____

Bible Reading

Reading: _____

Journaling Thoughts:
_____
_____
_____
_____
_____
_____
_____
_____
_____
_____
_____
_____

My Tasks:
_____ _____ _____
_____ _____ _____
_____ _____ _____

Today's Day/Date: _____ / _____

Prayer Time

Gratitude: What three things am I grateful for today?
_____
_____
_____

Confession: What sins do I need to confess?
_____
_____
_____

Requests: What am I praying for today?
_____
_____
_____

Bible Reading

Reading:
_____

Journaling Thoughts:
_____
_____
_____
_____
_____
_____
_____
_____
_____
_____
_____

My Tasks:

_____	_____	_____
_____	_____	_____
_____	_____	_____

Today's Day/Date: _____ / _____

Prayer Time

Gratitude: What three things am I grateful for today?
_____
_____
_____

Confession: What sins do I need to confess?
_____
_____
_____

Requests: What am I praying for today?
_____
_____
_____

Bible Reading

Reading:
_____

Journaling Thoughts:
_____
_____
_____
_____
_____
_____
_____
_____
_____
_____

My Tasks:
_____   _____   _____

_____   _____   _____

_____   _____   _____

Today's Day/Date: _____ / _____

Prayer Time

Gratitude: What three things am I grateful for today?
_____
_____
_____

Confession: What sins do I need to confess?
_____
_____
_____

Requests: What am I praying for today?
_____
_____
_____

Bible Reading

Reading:
_____

Journaling Thoughts:
_____
_____
_____
_____
_____
_____
_____
_____
_____
_____

My Tasks:
_____ _____ _____
_____ _____ _____
_____ _____ _____

Today's Day/Date: _____ / _____

Prayer Time

Gratitude: What three things am I grateful for today?
_____
_____
_____

Confession: What sins do I need to confess?
_____
_____
_____

Requests: What am I praying for today?
_____
_____
_____

Bible Reading

Reading:
_____

Journaling Thoughts:
_____
_____
_____
_____
_____
_____
_____
_____
_____
_____
_____

My Tasks:

_____	_____	_____
_____	_____	_____
_____	_____	_____

Today's Day/Date: _____ / _____

Prayer Time

Gratitude: What three things am I grateful for today?
_____
_____
_____

Confession: What sins do I need to confess?
_____
_____
_____

Requests: What am I praying for today?
_____
_____
_____

Bible Reading

Reading:
_____

Journaling Thoughts:
_____
_____
_____
_____
_____
_____
_____
_____
_____
_____

My Tasks:
_____ _____ _____

_____ _____ _____

_____ _____ _____

Today's Day/Date: _____ / _____

Prayer Time

Gratitude: What three things am I grateful for today?
_____
_____
_____

Confession: What sins do I need to confess?
_____
_____
_____

Requests: What am I praying for today?
_____
_____
_____

Bible Reading

Reading:
_____

Journaling Thoughts:
_____
_____
_____
_____
_____
_____
_____
_____
_____
_____

My Tasks:
_____   _____   _____

_____   _____   _____

_____   _____   _____

Today's Day/Date: _____ / _____

Prayer Time

Gratitude: What three things am I grateful for today?
_____
_____
_____

Confession: What sins do I need to confess?
_____
_____
_____

Requests: What am I praying for today?
_____
_____
_____

Bible Reading

Reading:
_____

Journaling Thoughts:
_____
_____
_____
_____
_____
_____
_____
_____
_____
_____
_____

My Tasks:

_____	_____	_____
_____	_____	_____
_____	_____	_____

Today's Day/Date: _____ / _____

Prayer Time

Gratitude: What three things am I grateful for today?
_____
_____
_____

Confession: What sins do I need to confess?
_____
_____
_____

Requests: What am I praying for today?
_____
_____
_____

Bible Reading

Reading:
_____

Journaling Thoughts:
_____
_____
_____
_____
_____
_____
_____
_____
_____
_____

My Tasks:
_____ _____ _____

_____ _____ _____

_____ _____ _____

Today's Day/Date: _____ / _____

Prayer Time

Gratitude: What three things am I grateful for today?
_____
_____
_____

Confession: What sins do I need to confess?
_____
_____
_____

Requests: What am I praying for today?
_____
_____
_____

Bible Reading

Reading:
_____

Journaling Thoughts:
_____
_____
_____
_____
_____
_____
_____
_____
_____
_____
_____

My Tasks:

_____	_____	_____
_____	_____	_____
_____	_____	_____

Today's Day/Date: _____ / _____

Prayer Time

Gratitude: What three things am I grateful for today?
_____
_____
_____

Confession: What sins do I need to confess?
_____
_____
_____

Requests: What am I praying for today?
_____
_____
_____

Bible Reading

Reading:
_____

Journaling Thoughts:
_____
_____
_____
_____
_____
_____
_____
_____
_____
_____

My Tasks:

_____	_____	_____
_____	_____	_____
_____	_____	_____

Today's Day/Date: _____ / _____

Prayer Time

Gratitude: What three things am I grateful for today?
_____
_____
_____

Confession: What sins do I need to confess?
_____
_____
_____

Requests: What am I praying for today?
_____
_____
_____

Bible Reading

Reading:
_____

Journaling Thoughts:
_____
_____
_____
_____
_____
_____
_____
_____
_____
_____
_____

My Tasks:

_____	_____	_____
_____	_____	_____
_____	_____	_____

Today's Day/Date: _____ / _____

Prayer Time

Gratitude: What three things am I grateful for today?
_____
_____
_____

Confession: What sins do I need to confess?
_____
_____
_____

Requests: What am I praying for today?
_____
_____
_____

Bible Reading

Reading:
_____

Journaling Thoughts:
_____
_____
_____
_____
_____
_____
_____
_____
_____
_____

My Tasks:
_____ _____ _____

_____ _____ _____

_____ _____ _____

Today's Day/Date: _____ / _____

Prayer Time

Gratitude: What three things am I grateful for today?
_____
_____
_____

Confession: What sins do I need to confess?
_____
_____
_____

Requests: What am I praying for today?
_____
_____
_____

Bible Reading

Reading:
_____

Journaling Thoughts:
_____
_____
_____
_____
_____
_____
_____
_____
_____
_____

My Tasks:

_____	_____	_____
_____	_____	_____
_____	_____	_____

Today's Day/Date: _____ / _____

Prayer Time

Gratitude: What three things am I grateful for today?
_____
_____
_____

Confession: What sins do I need to confess?
_____
_____
_____

Requests: What am I praying for today?
_____
_____
_____

Bible Reading

Reading:
_____

Journaling Thoughts:
_____
_____
_____
_____
_____
_____
_____
_____
_____

My Tasks:
_____   _____   _____

_____   _____   _____

_____   _____   _____

Today's Day/Date: _____ / _____

Prayer Time

Gratitude: What three things am I grateful for today?
_____
_____
_____

Confession: What sins do I need to confess?
_____
_____
_____

Requests: What am I praying for today?
_____
_____
_____

Bible Reading

Reading:
_____

Journaling Thoughts:
_____
_____
_____
_____
_____
_____
_____
_____
_____
_____
_____

My Tasks:

_____	_____	_____
_____	_____	_____
_____	_____	_____

Today's Day/Date: _____ / _____

Prayer Time

Gratitude: What three things am I grateful for today?
_____
_____
_____

Confession: What sins do I need to confess?
_____
_____
_____

Requests: What am I praying for today?
_____
_____
_____

Bible Reading

Reading:
_____

Journaling Thoughts:
_____
_____
_____
_____
_____
_____
_____
_____
_____
_____

My Tasks:
_____ _____ _____

_____ _____ _____

_____ _____ _____

Today's Day/Date: _____ / _____

Prayer Time

Gratitude: What three things am I grateful for today?
_____
_____
_____

Confession: What sins do I need to confess?
_____
_____
_____

Requests: What am I praying for today?
_____
_____
_____

Bible Reading

Reading:
_____

Journaling Thoughts:
_____
_____
_____
_____
_____
_____
_____
_____
_____
_____

My Tasks:

_____	_____	_____
_____	_____	_____
_____	_____	_____

Today's Day/Date: _____ / _____

Prayer Time

Gratitude: What three things am I grateful for today?
_____
_____
_____

Confession: What sins do I need to confess?
_____
_____
_____

Requests: What am I praying for today?
_____
_____
_____

Bible Reading

Reading:
_____

Journaling Thoughts:
_____
_____
_____
_____
_____
_____
_____
_____
_____
_____

My Tasks:

_____	_____	_____

_____	_____	_____

_____	_____	_____

Today's Day/Date: _____ / _____

Prayer Time

Gratitude: What three things am I grateful for today?
_____
_____
_____

Confession: What sins do I need to confess?
_____
_____
_____

Requests: What am I praying for today?
_____
_____
_____

Bible Reading

Reading:
_____

Journaling Thoughts:
_____
_____
_____
_____
_____
_____
_____
_____
_____
_____

My Tasks:

_____ _____ _____

_____ _____ _____

_____ _____ _____

Today's Day / Date: _____ / _____

Prayer Time

Gratitude: What three things am I grateful for today?
_____
_____
_____

Confession: What sins do I need to confess?
_____
_____
_____

Requests: What am I praying for today?
_____
_____
_____

Bible Reading

Reading:
_____

Journaling Thoughts:
_____
_____
_____
_____
_____
_____
_____
_____
_____
_____

My Tasks:
_____   _____   _____
_____   _____   _____
_____   _____   _____

Today's Day/Date: _____ / _____

Prayer Time

Gratitude: What three things am I grateful for today?
_____
_____
_____

Confession: What sins do I need to confess?
_____
_____
_____

Requests: What am I praying for today?
_____
_____
_____

Bible Reading

Reading:
_____

Journaling Thoughts:
_____
_____
_____
_____
_____
_____
_____
_____
_____
_____
_____

My Tasks:
_____	_____	_____
_____	_____	_____
_____	_____	_____

Today's Day/Date: _____ / _____

Prayer Time

Gratitude: What three things am I grateful for today?
_____
_____
_____

Confession: What sins do I need to confess?
_____
_____
_____

Requests: What am I praying for today?
_____
_____
_____

Bible Reading

Reading:
_____

Journaling Thoughts:
_____
_____
_____
_____
_____
_____
_____
_____
_____
_____

My Tasks:

_____   _____   _____

_____   _____   _____

_____   _____   _____

Today's Day / Date: _____ / _____

Prayer Time

Gratitude: What three things am I grateful for today?
_____
_____
_____

Confession: What sins do I need to confess?
_____
_____
_____

Requests: What am I praying for today?
_____
_____
_____

Bible Reading

Reading:
_____

Journaling Thoughts:
_____
_____
_____
_____
_____
_____
_____
_____
_____
_____
_____
_____

My Tasks:
_____   _____   _____

_____   _____   _____

_____   _____   _____

Today's Day/Date: _____ / _____

Prayer Time

Gratitude: What three things am I grateful for today?
_____
_____
_____

Confession: What sins do I need to confess?
_____
_____
_____

Requests: What am I praying for today?
_____
_____
_____

Bible Reading

Reading:
_____

Journaling Thoughts:
_____
_____
_____
_____
_____
_____
_____
_____
_____
_____

My Tasks:

_____	_____	_____
_____	_____	_____
_____	_____	_____

Today's Day/Date: _____ / _____

Prayer Time

Gratitude: What three things am I grateful for today?
_____
_____
_____

Confession: What sins do I need to confess?
_____
_____
_____

Requests: What am I praying for today?
_____
_____
_____

Bible Reading

Reading:
_____

Journaling Thoughts:
_____
_____
_____
_____
_____
_____
_____
_____
_____
_____

My Tasks:
_____ _____ _____

_____ _____ _____

_____ _____ _____

Today's Day/Date: _____ / _____

Prayer Time

Gratitude: What three things am I grateful for today?
_____
_____
_____

Confession: What sins do I need to confess?
_____
_____
_____

Requests: What am I praying for today?
_____
_____
_____

Bible Reading

Reading:
_____

Journaling Thoughts:
_____
_____
_____
_____
_____
_____
_____
_____
_____
_____

My Tasks:

_____	_____	_____
_____	_____	_____
_____	_____	_____

Today's Day/Date: _____ / _____

Prayer Time

Gratitude: What three things am I grateful for today?
_____
_____
_____

Confession: What sins do I need to confess?
_____
_____
_____

Requests: What am I praying for today?
_____
_____
_____

Bible Reading

Reading:
_____

Journaling Thoughts:
_____
_____
_____
_____
_____
_____
_____
_____
_____
_____

My Tasks:
_____ _____ _____

_____ _____ _____

_____ _____ _____

Today's Day/Date: _____ / _____

Prayer Time

Gratitude: What three things am I grateful for today?
_____
_____
_____

Confession: What sins do I need to confess?
_____
_____
_____

Requests: What am I praying for today?
_____
_____
_____

Bible Reading

Reading:
_____

Journaling Thoughts:
_____
_____
_____
_____
_____
_____
_____
_____
_____
_____
_____

My Tasks:

_____	_____	_____
_____	_____	_____
_____	_____	_____

Today's Day/Date: _____ / _____

Prayer Time

Gratitude: What three things am I grateful for today?
_____
_____
_____

Confession: What sins do I need to confess?
_____
_____
_____

Requests: What am I praying for today?
_____
_____
_____

Bible Reading

Reading:
_____

Journaling Thoughts:
_____
_____
_____
_____
_____
_____
_____
_____
_____
_____
_____

My Tasks:
_____ _____ _____
_____ _____ _____
_____ _____ _____

Today's Day / Date: _____ / _____

Prayer Time

Gratitude: What three things am I grateful for today?
_____
_____
_____

Confession: What sins do I need to confess?
_____
_____
_____

Requests: What am I praying for today?
_____
_____
_____

Bible Reading

Reading:
_____

Journaling Thoughts:
_____
_____
_____
_____
_____
_____
_____
_____
_____
_____

My Tasks:
_____ _____ _____

_____ _____ _____

_____ _____ _____

Today's Day/Date: _____ / _____

Prayer Time

Gratitude: What three things am I grateful for today?
_____
_____
_____

Confession: What sins do I need to confess?
_____
_____
_____

Requests: What am I praying for today?
_____
_____
_____

Bible Reading

Reading:
_____

Journaling Thoughts:
_____
_____
_____
_____
_____
_____
_____
_____
_____
_____

My Tasks:

_____	_____	_____
_____	_____	_____
_____	_____	_____

Today's Day/Date: _____ / _____

Prayer Time

Gratitude: What three things am I grateful for today?
_____
_____
_____

Confession: What sins do I need to confess?
_____
_____
_____

Requests: What am I praying for today?
_____
_____
_____

Bible Reading

Reading:
_____

Journaling Thoughts:
_____
_____
_____
_____
_____
_____
_____
_____
_____
_____
_____

My Tasks:

_____	_____	_____
_____	_____	_____
_____	_____	_____

Today's Day/Date: _____ / _____

Prayer Time

Gratitude: What three things am I grateful for today?
_____
_____
_____

Confession: What sins do I need to confess?
_____
_____
_____

Requests: What am I praying for today?
_____
_____
_____

Bible Reading

Reading:
_____

Journaling Thoughts:
_____
_____
_____
_____
_____
_____
_____
_____
_____
_____

My Tasks:

_____   _____   _____

_____   _____   _____

_____   _____   _____

Today's Day / Date: _____ / _____

Prayer Time

Gratitude: What three things am I grateful for today?
_____
_____
_____

Confession: What sins do I need to confess?
_____
_____
_____

Requests: What am I praying for today?
_____
_____
_____

Bible Reading

Reading:
_____

Journaling Thoughts:
_____
_____
_____
_____
_____
_____
_____
_____
_____
_____

My Tasks:
_____	_____	_____
_____	_____	_____
_____	_____	_____

Today's Day/Date: _____ / _____

Prayer Time

Gratitude: What three things am I grateful for today?
_____
_____
_____

Confession: What sins do I need to confess?
_____
_____
_____

Requests: What am I praying for today?
_____
_____
_____

Bible Reading

Reading:
_____

Journaling Thoughts:
_____
_____
_____
_____
_____
_____
_____
_____
_____
_____

My Tasks:
_____   _____   _____

_____   _____   _____

_____   _____   _____

Today's Day/Date: _____ / _____

Prayer Time

Gratitude: What three things am I grateful for today?
_____
_____
_____

Confession: What sins do I need to confess?
_____
_____
_____

Requests: What am I praying for today?
_____
_____
_____

Bible Reading

Reading:
_____

Journaling Thoughts:
_____
_____
_____
_____
_____
_____
_____
_____
_____
_____

My Tasks:
_____ _____ _____
_____ _____ _____
_____ _____ _____

Today's Day/Date: _____ / _____

Prayer Time

Gratitude: What three things am I grateful for today?
_____
_____
_____

Confession: What sins do I need to confess?
_____
_____
_____

Requests: What am I praying for today?
_____
_____
_____

Bible Reading

Reading:
_____

Journaling Thoughts:
_____
_____
_____
_____
_____
_____
_____
_____
_____
_____

My Tasks:

_____ _____ _____

_____ _____ _____

_____ _____ _____

Today's Day/Date: _____ / _____

Prayer Time

Gratitude: What three things am I grateful for today?
_____
_____
_____

Confession: What sins do I need to confess?
_____
_____
_____

Requests: What am I praying for today?
_____
_____
_____

Bible Reading

Reading:
_____

Journaling Thoughts:
_____
_____
_____
_____
_____
_____
_____
_____
_____
_____

My Tasks:

| _____ | _____ | _____ |
| _____ | _____ | _____ |

Today's Day/Date: _____ / _____

Prayer Time

Gratitude: What three things am I grateful for today?
_____
_____
_____

Confession: What sins do I need to confess?
_____
_____
_____

Requests: What am I praying for today?
_____
_____
_____

Bible Reading

Reading:
_____

Journaling Thoughts:
_____
_____
_____
_____
_____
_____
_____
_____
_____
_____

My Tasks:
_____ _____ _____
_____ _____ _____
_____ _____ _____

Today's Day/Date: _____ / _____

Prayer Time

Gratitude: What three things am I grateful for today?
_____
_____
_____

Confession: What sins do I need to confess?
_____
_____
_____

Requests: What am I praying for today?
_____
_____
_____

Bible Reading

Reading:
_____

Journaling Thoughts:
_____
_____
_____
_____
_____
_____
_____
_____
_____
_____

My Tasks:
_____ _____ _____

_____ _____ _____

_____ _____ _____

Today's Day/Date: _____ / _____

Prayer Time

Gratitude: What three things am I grateful for today?
_____
_____
_____

Confession: What sins do I need to confess?
_____
_____
_____

Requests: What am I praying for today?
_____
_____
_____

Bible Reading

Reading:
_____

Journaling Thoughts:
_____
_____
_____
_____
_____
_____
_____
_____
_____
_____

My Tasks:

_____	_____	_____
_____	_____	_____
_____	_____	_____

Today's Day/Date: _____ / _____

Prayer Time

Gratitude: What three things am I grateful for today?
_____
_____
_____

Confession: What sins do I need to confess?
_____
_____
_____

Requests: What am I praying for today?
_____
_____
_____

Bible Reading

Reading:
_____

Journaling Thoughts:
_____
_____
_____
_____
_____
_____
_____
_____
_____
_____

My Tasks:

| _____ | _____ | _____ |
| _____ | _____ | _____ |

Today's Day/Date: _____ / _____

Prayer Time

Gratitude: What three things am I grateful for today?
_____
_____
_____

Confession: What sins do I need to confess?
_____
_____
_____

Requests: What am I praying for today?
_____
_____
_____

Bible Reading

Reading:
_____

Journaling Thoughts:
_____
_____
_____
_____
_____
_____
_____
_____
_____
_____
_____

My Tasks:

_____	_____	_____
_____	_____	_____
_____	_____	_____

Today's Day/Date: _____ / _____

Prayer Time

Gratitude: What three things am I grateful for today?
_____
_____
_____

Confession: What sins do I need to confess?
_____
_____
_____

Requests: What am I praying for today?
_____
_____
_____

Bible Reading

Reading: _____

Journaling Thoughts:
_____
_____
_____
_____
_____
_____
_____
_____
_____
_____

My Tasks:
_____ _____ _____

_____ _____ _____

_____ _____ _____

Today's Day / Date: _____ / _____

Prayer Time

Gratitude: What three things am I grateful for today?
_____
_____
_____

Confession: What sins do I need to confess?
_____
_____
_____

Requests: What am I praying for today?
_____
_____
_____

Bible Reading

Reading:
_____

Journaling Thoughts:
_____
_____
_____
_____
_____
_____
_____
_____
_____
_____

My Tasks:

_____   _____   _____

_____   _____   _____

_____   _____   _____

Today's Day/Date: _____ / _____

Prayer Time

Gratitude: What three things am I grateful for today?
_____
_____
_____

Confession: What sins do I need to confess?
_____
_____
_____

Requests: What am I praying for today?
_____
_____
_____

Bible Reading

Reading:
_____

Journaling Thoughts:
_____
_____
_____
_____
_____
_____
_____
_____
_____
_____

My Tasks:

_____ _____ _____

_____ _____ _____

_____ _____ _____

Today's Day/Date: _____ / _____

Prayer Time

Gratitude: What three things am I grateful for today?
_____
_____
_____

Confession: What sins do I need to confess?
_____
_____
_____

Requests: What am I praying for today?
_____
_____
_____

Bible Reading

Reading:
_____

Journaling Thoughts:
_____
_____
_____
_____
_____
_____
_____
_____
_____
_____
_____

My Tasks:

_____	_____	_____
_____	_____	_____
_____	_____	_____

Today's Day/Date: _____ / _____

Prayer Time

Gratitude: What three things am I grateful for today?
_____
_____
_____

Confession: What sins do I need to confess?
_____
_____
_____

Requests: What am I praying for today?
_____
_____
_____

Bible Reading

Reading:
_____

Journaling Thoughts:
_____
_____
_____
_____
_____
_____
_____
_____
_____
_____

My Tasks:

_____	_____	_____
_____	_____	_____
_____	_____	_____

Today's Day/Date: _____ / _____

Prayer Time

Gratitude: What three things am I grateful for today?
_____
_____
_____

Confession: What sins do I need to confess?
_____
_____
_____

Requests: What am I praying for today?
_____
_____
_____

Bible Reading

Reading:
_____

Journaling Thoughts:
_____
_____
_____
_____
_____
_____
_____
_____
_____
_____

My Tasks:
_____ _____ _____

_____ _____ _____

_____ _____ _____

Today's Day / Date: _____ / _____

Prayer Time

Gratitude: What three things am I grateful for today?
_____
_____
_____

Confession: What sins do I need to confess?
_____
_____
_____

Requests: What am I praying for today?
_____
_____
_____

Bible Reading

Reading:
_____

Journaling Thoughts:
_____
_____
_____
_____
_____
_____
_____
_____
_____
_____

My Tasks:

_____	_____	_____
_____	_____	_____
_____	_____	_____

Today's Day / Date: _____ / _____

Prayer Time

Gratitude: What three things am I grateful for today?
_____
_____
_____

Confession: What sins do I need to confess?
_____
_____
_____

Requests: What am I praying for today?
_____
_____
_____

Bible Reading

Reading:
_____

Journaling Thoughts:
_____
_____
_____
_____
_____
_____
_____
_____
_____
_____

My Tasks:

_____	_____	_____
_____	_____	_____
_____	_____	_____

Today's Day/Date: _____ / _____

Prayer Time

Gratitude: What three things am I grateful for today?
_____
_____
_____

Confession: What sins do I need to confess?
_____
_____
_____

Requests: What am I praying for today?
_____
_____
_____

Bible Reading

Reading:
_____

Journaling Thoughts:
_____
_____
_____
_____
_____
_____
_____
_____
_____
_____

My Tasks:

_____	_____	_____
_____	_____	_____
_____	_____	_____

Today's Day/Date: _____ / _____

Prayer Time

Gratitude: What three things am I grateful for today?
_____
_____
_____

Confession: What sins do I need to confess?
_____
_____
_____

Requests: What am I praying for today?
_____
_____
_____

Bible Reading

Reading:
_____

Journaling Thoughts:
_____
_____
_____
_____
_____
_____
_____
_____
_____
_____

My Tasks:

_____ _____ _____

_____ _____ _____

_____ _____ _____

Today's Day/Date: _____ / _____

Prayer Time

Gratitude: What three things am I grateful for today?
_____
_____
_____

Confession: What sins do I need to confess?
_____
_____
_____

Requests: What am I praying for today?
_____
_____
_____

Bible Reading

Reading:
_____

Journaling Thoughts:
_____
_____
_____
_____
_____
_____
_____
_____
_____
_____
_____

My Tasks:
_____ _____ _____
_____ _____ _____
_____ _____ _____

Today's Day / Date: _____ / _____

Prayer Time

Gratitude: What three things am I grateful for today?
_____
_____
_____

Confession: What sins do I need to confess?
_____
_____
_____

Requests: What am I praying for today?
_____
_____
_____

Bible Reading

Reading:
_____

Journaling Thoughts:
_____
_____
_____
_____
_____
_____
_____
_____
_____
_____
_____

My Tasks:

_____	_____	_____
_____	_____	_____
_____	_____	_____

Today's Day/Date: _____ / _____

Prayer Time

Gratitude: What three things am I grateful for today?
_____
_____
_____

Confession: What sins do I need to confess?
_____
_____
_____

Requests: What am I praying for today?
_____
_____
_____

Bible Reading

Reading:
_____

Journaling Thoughts:
_____
_____
_____
_____
_____
_____
_____
_____
_____
_____

My Tasks:
_____ _____ _____
_____ _____ _____
_____ _____ _____

Today's Day/Date: _____ / _____

Prayer Time

Gratitude: What three things am I grateful for today?
_____
_____
_____

Confession: What sins do I need to confess?
_____
_____
_____

Requests: What am I praying for today?
_____
_____
_____

Bible Reading

Reading:
_____

Journaling Thoughts:
_____
_____
_____
_____
_____
_____
_____
_____
_____
_____
_____

My Tasks:
_____	_____	_____
_____	_____	_____
_____	_____	_____

Today's Day/Date: _____ / _____

Prayer Time

Gratitude: What three things am I grateful for today?
_____
_____
_____

Confession: What sins do I need to confess?
_____
_____
_____

Requests: What am I praying for today?
_____
_____
_____

Bible Reading

Reading:
_____

Journaling Thoughts:
_____
_____
_____
_____
_____
_____
_____
_____
_____
_____

My Tasks:
_____	_____	_____
_____	_____	_____
_____	_____	_____

Today's Day / Date: _____ / _____

Prayer Time

Gratitude: What three things am I grateful for today?
_____
_____
_____

Confession: What sins do I need to confess?
_____
_____
_____

Requests: What am I praying for today?
_____
_____
_____

Bible Reading

Reading:
_____

Journaling Thoughts:
_____
_____
_____
_____
_____
_____
_____
_____
_____
_____

My Tasks:

_____   _____   _____

_____   _____   _____

_____   _____   _____

Today's Day/Date: _____ / _____

Prayer Time

Gratitude: What three things am I grateful for today?
_____
_____
_____

Confession: What sins do I need to confess?
_____
_____
_____

Requests: What am I praying for today?
_____
_____
_____

Bible Reading

Reading:
_____

Journaling Thoughts:
_____
_____
_____
_____
_____
_____
_____
_____
_____
_____

My Tasks:
_____ _____ _____
_____ _____ _____
_____ _____ _____

Today's Day/Date: _____ / _____

Prayer Time

Gratitude: What three things am I grateful for today?
_____
_____
_____

Confession: What sins do I need to confess?
_____
_____
_____

Requests: What am I praying for today?
_____
_____
_____

Bible Reading

Reading:
_____

Journaling Thoughts:
_____
_____
_____
_____
_____
_____
_____
_____
_____
_____

My Tasks:
_____ _____ _____

_____ _____ _____

_____ _____ _____

Today's Day / Date: _____ / _____

Prayer Time

Gratitude: What three things am I grateful for today?
_____
_____
_____

Confession: What sins do I need to confess?
_____
_____
_____

Requests: What am I praying for today?
_____
_____
_____

Bible Reading

Reading:
_____

Journaling Thoughts:
_____
_____
_____
_____
_____
_____
_____
_____
_____
_____

My Tasks:

_____ _____ _____

_____ _____ _____

Today's Day/Date: _____ / _____

Prayer Time

Gratitude: What three things am I grateful for today?
_____
_____
_____

Confession: What sins do I need to confess?
_____
_____
_____

Requests: What am I praying for today?
_____
_____
_____

Bible Reading

Reading:
_____

Journaling Thoughts:
_____
_____
_____
_____
_____
_____
_____
_____
_____
_____
_____

My Tasks:

_____	_____	_____
_____	_____	_____
_____	_____	_____

Today's Day / Date: _____ / _____

Prayer Time

Gratitude: What three things am I grateful for today?
_____
_____
_____

Confession: What sins do I need to confess?
_____
_____
_____

Requests: What am I praying for today?
_____
_____
_____

Bible Reading

Reading: _____

Journaling Thoughts:
_____
_____
_____
_____
_____
_____
_____
_____
_____
_____

My Tasks:

_____	_____	_____
_____	_____	_____
_____	_____	_____

Today's Day/Date: _____ / _____

Prayer Time

Gratitude: What three things am I grateful for today?
_____
_____
_____

Confession: What sins do I need to confess?
_____
_____
_____

Requests: What am I praying for today?
_____
_____
_____

Bible Reading

Reading:
_____

Journaling Thoughts:
_____
_____
_____
_____
_____
_____
_____
_____
_____
_____
_____

My Tasks:
_____ _____ _____
_____ _____ _____
_____ _____ _____

Today's Day/Date: _____ / _____

Prayer Time

Gratitude: What three things am I grateful for today?
_____
_____
_____

Confession: What sins do I need to confess?
_____
_____
_____

Requests: What am I praying for today?
_____
_____
_____

Bible Reading

Reading:
_____

Journaling Thoughts:
_____
_____
_____
_____
_____
_____
_____
_____
_____
_____

My Tasks:
_____ _____ _____
_____ _____ _____
_____ _____ _____

Today's Day/Date: _____ / _____

Prayer Time

Gratitude: What three things am I grateful for today?
_____
_____
_____

Confession: What sins do I need to confess?
_____
_____
_____

Requests: What am I praying for today?
_____
_____
_____

Bible Reading

Reading:
_____

Journaling Thoughts:
_____
_____
_____
_____
_____
_____
_____
_____
_____
_____

My Tasks:
_____ _____ _____

_____ _____ _____

_____ _____ _____

Today's Day/Date: _____ / _____

Prayer Time

Gratitude: What three things am I grateful for today?
_____
_____
_____

Confession: What sins do I need to confess?
_____
_____
_____

Requests: What am I praying for today?
_____
_____
_____

Bible Reading

Reading:
_____

Journaling Thoughts:
_____
_____
_____
_____
_____
_____
_____
_____
_____
_____
_____

My Tasks:
_____   _____   _____

_____   _____   _____

_____   _____   _____

Today's Day/Date: _____ / _____

Prayer Time

Gratitude: What three things am I grateful for today?
_____
_____
_____

Confession: What sins do I need to confess?
_____
_____
_____

Requests: What am I praying for today?
_____
_____
_____

Bible Reading

Reading:
_____

Journaling Thoughts:
_____
_____
_____
_____
_____
_____
_____
_____
_____
_____

My Tasks:
_____   _____   _____

_____   _____   _____

_____   _____   _____

Today's Day/Date: _____ / _____

Prayer Time

Gratitude: What three things am I grateful for today?
_____
_____
_____

Confession: What sins do I need to confess?
_____
_____
_____

Requests: What am I praying for today?
_____
_____
_____

Bible Reading

Reading:
_____

Journaling Thoughts:
_____
_____
_____
_____
_____
_____
_____
_____
_____
_____

My Tasks:

_____	_____	_____
_____	_____	_____
_____	_____	_____

Today's Day / Date: _____ / _____

Prayer Time

Gratitude: What three things am I grateful for today?
_____
_____
_____

Confession: What sins do I need to confess?
_____
_____
_____

Requests: What am I praying for today?
_____
_____
_____

Bible Reading

Reading:
_____

Journaling Thoughts:
_____
_____
_____
_____
_____
_____
_____
_____
_____
_____

My Tasks:

_____ _____ _____

_____ _____ _____

_____ _____ _____

Today's Day/Date: _____ / _____

Prayer Time

Gratitude: What three things am I grateful for today?
_____
_____
_____

Confession: What sins do I need to confess?
_____
_____
_____

Requests: What am I praying for today?
_____
_____
_____

Bible Reading

Reading:
_____

Journaling Thoughts:
_____
_____
_____
_____
_____
_____
_____
_____
_____
_____

My Tasks:
_____ _____ _____
_____ _____ _____
_____ _____ _____

Today's Day/Date: _____ / _____

Prayer Time

Gratitude: What three things am I grateful for today?
_____
_____
_____

Confession: What sins do I need to confess?
_____
_____
_____

Requests: What am I praying for today?
_____
_____
_____

Bible Reading

Reading:
_____

Journaling Thoughts:
_____
_____
_____
_____
_____
_____
_____
_____
_____
_____

My Tasks:
_____   _____   _____

_____   _____   _____

_____   _____   _____

Today's Day/Date: _____ / _____

Prayer Time

Gratitude: What three things am I grateful for today?
_____
_____
_____

Confession: What sins do I need to confess?
_____
_____
_____

Requests: What am I praying for today?
_____
_____
_____

Bible Reading

Reading: _____

Journaling Thoughts:
_____
_____
_____
_____
_____
_____
_____
_____
_____
_____

My Tasks:

_____	_____	_____
_____	_____	_____
_____	_____	_____

Today's Day / Date: _____ / _____

Prayer Time

Gratitude: What three things am I grateful for today?
_____
_____
_____

Confession: What sins do I need to confess?
_____
_____
_____

Requests: What am I praying for today?
_____
_____
_____

Bible Reading

Reading:
_____

Journaling Thoughts:
_____
_____
_____
_____
_____
_____
_____
_____
_____
_____
_____

My Tasks:

_____   _____   _____

_____   _____   _____

_____   _____   _____